Gilgamesh Retold

JENNY LEWIS is an Anglo-Welsh poet, playwright, songwriter, children's author and translator who teaches poetry at Oxford University. She trained as a painter at the Ruskin School of Art before reading English at St Edmund Hall, Oxford. She has worked as an advertising copywriter and a government press officer for, among others, the Equality and Human Rights Commission. She has also written children's books and plays and co-written, with its creator, Kate Canning, a twenty-six-part children's TV animation series, *James the Cat*. Her first poetry sequence, *When I Became an Amazon* (Iron Press, 1996) was broadcast on BBC *Woman's Hour*, translated into Russian (Bilingua, 2002) and made into an opera with music by Gennadyi Shizoglazov which had its world premiere with the Tchaikovsky Opera and Ballet Company in Perm, Russia, November 2017. Since 2012, Jenny has been working with the Iraqi poet Adnan al-Sayegh on an award-winning Arts Council-funded project, 'Writing Mesopotamia', which aims to build bridges and foster friendships between English and Arabic-speaking communities. Her work for the theatre includes *Map of Stars* (2002), *Garden of the Senses* (2005), *After Gilgamesh* (2011) and, with Yasmin Sidhwa and Adnan al-Sayegh, *Stories for Survival: a Re-telling of the 1001, Arabian Nights* (2015). She has published two collections with Oxford Poets/Carcanet, *Fathom* (2007) and *Taking Mesopotamia* (2014). Jenny is currently completing a PhD on *Gilgamesh* at Goldsmiths.

CARCANET CLASSICS INCLUDE

Dictator/Gilgamesh adapted by Philip Terry
Beowulf by Chris McCully
Pearl translated by Jane Draycott
Edmund Blunden *Selected Poems* edited by Robyn Marsack
Catullus *The Books of Catullus* edited and translated by Simon Smith
Rebecca Elson *A Responsibility to Awe: Collected Poems*
edited by Anne Berkeley, Angelo di Cintio and Bernard O'Donoghue
John Heath-Stubbs *Selected Poems* edited by John Clegg
Walter Pater *Selected Essays* edited by Alex Wong
Propertius *Poems* translated by James Womack
Arthur Rimbaud *Illuminations* translated by John Ashbery
George Seferis *Collected Poems* translated by Edmund Keeley
and Philip Sherrard
Charles Tomlinson *Swimming Chenango Lake: selected poems*
edited by David Morley
William Carlos Williams *Collected Poems volumes I and II*
edited by A. Walton Litz and Christopher MacGowan

JENNY LEWIS

GILGAMESH RETOLD

A response to the ancient epic

Carcanet Classics

MMXVIII

First published in Great Britain in 2018 by
Carcanet
Alliance House, 30 Cross Street
Manchester M2 7AQ
www.carcanet.co.uk

A CIP catalogue record for this book is available from the British Library,
ISBN 978 1 78410 614 0

Typeset by Andrew Latimer in Jenson
Printed in Great Britain by SRP Ltd., Exeter, Devon

The publisher acknowledges financial assistance from Arts Council England.

Here is the epic of the fear of death.

— RAINER MARIA RILKE

To my grandmother

EMILY MAUD KENT

1878–1970

Contents

Gilgamesh Retold

Preface

Stories evolve to suit contemporary tastes and each retelling must create its own unity in the mind of the storyteller before it can achieve coherence for the reader. Because of this I describe *Gilgamesh Retold* as my response to its original source, the Mesopotamian *Epic of Gilgamesh*. Early Sumerian poems concerning King Gilgamesh of Uruk started to be written down between 2100–1750 BC and were circulated orally long before that. This book tells the story in fifteen chapters, with a prologue and epilogue, using different poetic forms to suggest the telling in different voices. It was mainly inspired by episodes from tablets one to eleven of the standard twelve tablet version collated by the priest-scribe-exorcist Sin-lique-uninni in around 1200 BC. This great cornerstone of world literature, written in cuneiform on clay tablets, was discovered in the mid-nineteenth century by archaeologists excavating the buried library of the Assyrian king, Ashurbanipal (668–627 BC). Some recently deciphered tablets tell the story differently or add previously unrecorded details, giving the *Epic of Gilgamesh* a vigorous sense of life continuing beyond the covers of existing books.

List of Characters

Gilgamesh, King of Uruk (pronounced Gil GA mesh)
Enkidu, Gilgamesh's close friend and companion (pronounced En KI du)
Ninsun, a minor goddess and Gilgamesh's mother
Aruru, the goddess of fertility who protects pregnant women
Shamash, the sun god
Aya, the goddess of dawn and Shamash's bride
Shamhat, a *hierodule* or 'sacred prostitute' in service at the temple of the goddess Inanna
Inanna, the goddess of love, sex and fertility – Uruk's ruling deity. In her later, more ferocious manifestation she was known as Ishtar, goddess of love, sex and war
Humbaba, an ogre appointed by the deities to guard the cedar forest
Anu, a principal deity and father of Inanna/Ishtar
Enlil, the god of wind, air, earth and storms, the second principal deity with Anu and Ea
Ea, the god of water who resides in the ocean under the earth known as the *abzu*
Erishkagel, Inanna's sister, queen of the underworld
Belet-Seri, a minor goddess who resides in the underworld, giving Erishkagel an account of all the souls who pass through the gates
Siduri, a minor goddess and wise woman
Ur-shanabi, the boatman who ferries Gilgamesh across the Sea of Death
Uta-napishtim, the Flood survivor
Uta-napishtim's wife
Zaqar, conveyor of dreams and messenger of the moon god, Sin
Hunter
Barber
Wedding Guests
Shepherds
Citizens of Uruk
Scorpion man and woman

Babylonian Words

Eme-sal: women's language (see chapter twelve, and a discussion in the Afterword)

Gidim-xul: evil ghost or tormentor (see chapter fourteen)

Eanna: the ancient Sumerian temple and area around it, dedicated to Inanna (see chapter fifteen)

Map of Gilgamesh's Mesopotamia (Mesopotamia means 'between rivers'), showing his city, Uruk, the rivers Tigris and Euphrates and the conjectured location of the cedar forest. Earlier Sumerian versions of the *Epic of Gilgamesh* say that Gilgamesh travelled east to the cedar forest, yet the later more extensive Babylonian examples place the cedar forests west in Lebanon.

Prologue

Gilgamesh knew   he understood
        how the waters broke   how the world was birthed
the weight of life   heavy as a flood
        the full womb   the still grave

He sensed secrets   guarded by gods
        wandered wide   told a tale
dreaded death   longed for light
        found and lost   his first love

Often he travelled   Shamash's warrior
        just as the sun god   circles the earth
Gilgamesh built   the wall of Uruk
        a strong strand   circling his city

See these bricks   from river mud
        the rustle of reeds   in winter is in them
the hubbub of storms   in summer is in them
        the smell of Euphrates   and Tigris is in them

As many bricks   as birds fly west
        dried to hardness   on Uruk's roofs
creating a temple   for holy Inanna
        and inside the temple   a casket of cedar

Inside the cedar   the memory of forests
        where Enkidu ran   with his herd of gazelles
where Gilgamesh fought   the giant Humbaba
        to bring back wood   to the city of Uruk

Read it now   here on the page
his own story   told by the tribe
of Gilgamesh   at the Edge of the World
of Gilgamesh   on the Waters of Death

How he found   the Flood survivor
in a far place   found Uta-napishtim
how he greeted   the goddess Siduri
how he lost   his life-giving plant

Mighty and handsome   a glorious hero
unmatched in combat   none could defeat him
his people kept safe   in the sheepfold of Uruk
surpassing all kings   his name is a legend

I

The Coming of Enkidu

Gilgamesh, King of Uruk, is two-thirds god and one-third human. He is also a tyrant and oppressor. In despair, his people ask the deities for help. The goddess Aruru makes a wild man from spit and mud to tame Gilgamesh.

A hurricane moved | the mind of Gilgamesh
Tornado of tantrums | he shattered the city
Even his mother | veiled her face
Even the gods | were goaded to gall.

At last they called | the goddess Aruru
Fertile womb goddess | who made the first humans
She made life spurt | from the mud of the river
She made life spring | from the clay of the uplands.

The great Aruru | knew the right answer
To fashion a man | equal to Gilgamesh
An untamed man | to tame the tyrant
An untaught man | to teach him secrets.

Out of the silence | out of the sunlight
Out of the shadows | that carpet the forest
Stepped a man, beautiful | strong like an eagle
Stepped a man, god-like | lithe as a lion.

His hair rolled down | like waves of a torrent
His beard luxuriant | bushy as barley
Dense and waving | the hair of his body
Like an animal god | he stood in the forest.

A grazing animal | joining his herd
Gazelles ran round him | down to the water-hole
He ran with the animals | down to the water-hole
This was Enkidu | made for Gilgamesh.

A hunter saw him | saw him by chance
Gazelles running freely | Enkidu with them
A giant was Enkidu | naked and powerful
Lord of Wild Nature | protecting his beasts.

The hunter crouched | quiet in the moonlight
Secretly watched | from safety of shadows
This was the wolf-man | emptying his traps
This was the wild-dog | springing his snares.

Angry and fearful | he travelled to Uruk
Told Gilgamesh | who listened with care
Commanded the hunter | to tell him each detail
He'd seen Enkidu | before in a dream.

Gilgamesh frowned | said to the hunter
'Go quickly and find | the hierodule Shamhat
Like a gazelle | she waits in the temple
Offering herself | in Inanna's service.

Take her with you | to the place in the forest
The place where the wild man | drinks from the lake
Tell her to lie | undressed by the water-hole
She must be naked | a beautiful snare.

Once they've had sex | his herd will desert him
Once he has known | the bliss of her body
He'll want to follow her | out of the forest
Follow her back | to the city of Uruk.'

Three days they walked | the hunter and Shamhat
Away from the city | out into the country
Three more they waited | there by the water-hole
Waiting to lure | the wild man Enkidu.

Shamhat was sitting | quiet by the pool's edge
Watching the flickering | fish in the shallows
When suddenly Enkidu | stood there before her
She took in his odour | of forest and hillside.

The hierodule gasped | as he bent to touch her
Stroking her hair | like the fur of an animal
Stroking her thighs | like the flanks of an animal
As he caressed her | he sang to her softly.

Inanna looked down | blessing the lovers
Six days, seven nights | their bodies were joined
Six days, seven nights | their flesh was one flesh
Six days, seven nights | their souls were one soul.

On day number seven | they rested together
Then Enkidu set off | to re-join his herd
But now gazelles ran | flung fearful glances
Hoof-beats soon distant | a patter of thunder.

Slowly he came back | sat down by Shamhat
There by the lake | they started to talk
'Why not come back | with me to the city
Open your eyes | to the splendours of Uruk.

All day, you'll find | there is singing and dancing
Tambours and cymbals | reed pipes and lyres
Come to the temple | of blessed Inanna
See golden statues | and tablets of lapis.

And there's Gilgamesh | manly and handsome
Even taller than you | even stronger, more virile
His hair thick as yours | like a field of ripe barley
Eyes dark as wine | at the base of a pitcher.'

Enkidu thought | of his life in the forest
Untamed and free | yet lonely and friendless
Should he go now | to the city with Shamhat?
Follow the hierodule | back to the city?

2

'He Saw You in Dreams...'

Shamhat tells Enkidu that Gilgamesh is waiting for him.

Then Shamhat said, 'He first saw you in dreams,
Saw you before he'd ever heard of you.
In the first, while watching stars, it seems
One lost its grip, and hurtling closer, grew
Gigantic, landed with such force between
The Tigris and Euphrates that a new
Crater was formed that was much larger than
The salty Sawa lake or Saturn's moon.

People crowded round it in a flock,
Wanted to kiss it, like a baby's feet.
They knelt and prayed before this piece of rock
In case it brought them luck or changed their fate,
But Gilgamesh is made from stronger stock –
He put his shoulder underneath the great
Meteorite, and like a little boy,
He lifted it as if it were a toy.

The goddess Ninsun, Gilgamesh's mother,
Explained her understanding of the dream –
A man was coming to him, a new brother,
To love and protect Gilgamesh and seem
More of a soul-mate than a friend, another
Entity that, parted in the stream
At birth, had found its own way back to meet
Itself again – and make itself complete.

The second dream was in Uruk's main square –
A multitude of people clustered round
An axe forged in the palace blacksmith's fire

Its bulk so huge it covered all the ground
Between Inanna's temple and the far-
Off river bank. Then Gilgamesh bent down
And with a dreadful groan, he picked it up
And carried it to Ninsun, every step

Surrounded by the cheering crowd who threw
Themselves before him as he made his way
In triumph to the palace. Now they knew
Their leader was a god, and knelt to pray
And give him thanks, while goddess Ninsun drew
Gilgamesh to her saying, "Soon the day
Approaches when at last you'll meet this man.
He'll love and guard you like no other can.'"

3

Enkidu's Decision

Shamhat continues to persuade Enkidu to come back with her to Uruk.

Later that day, she turned to him and said
'Like Gilgamesh you have a god-like image.
Why show your beauty only to your herd?

Year after year, why be content to forage
In the woods, a lonely soul, until,
like creeping undergrowth, the pains of age

fetter your body with a numbing chill
and you expire unknown beneath some tree
with nobody to mourn you but an owl?

Come to Uruk now and you will see
A world of wonders that will make you stare
At every turn; a hive, a tapestry

Alive with colours; in the temple square
Exorcists, dancers, eunuchs, priestesses
Mix with more humble souls who travel there

To offer sacrifices to the goddess,
Great Inanna, who is Uruk's queen.
And lining all the streets and terraces

Tall citrus trees and date palms cast a green
And welcome shade from Shamash's strong rays
Which, glimmering through leaves, still catch the sheen

Of gold on parapets and balconies.
Each person carries out their skill or trade:
And here you'll also find your rightful place.'

The forest with its gritty footpaths made
A sound as if it shifted on its bed
And hung its heavy canopy, afraid

Of portents in the wind, and what she said;
Of how the sunset turned the river red;
Of how there was a sudden smell of blood.

4

Enkidu and Gilgamesh

Finally persuaded by Shamhat, Enkidu decides to travel to Uruk to meet Gilgamesh. On the way they stop at a shepherd's camp.

Ahead were hills that leaned against the sky
At first dark green, then pale and paler still
And wooded valleys, echoing with birds,
With coils of mist that thinned then fell away
Allowing beams of light to drape the land.
For the first time Enkidu saw it all –
Expanses spread before his narrowed eyes
Not flecked with shade like his known forest paths
But all laid bare and open in the sun.
They travelled on, and when at last the moon
Rose high above the distant citadels
They smelt the scent of herbs and roasting lamb
And saw the firelight of a shepherd's camp.
Along the path they met a shepherd boy
Who led them to the camp and sat them down
Around the fire and brought them bread and beer.
First one, then two, then three, then four, then five,
Then six, then seven jugs Enkidu downed
Then laughed, and as his monstrous shadow shrank
And lengthened with the flickering of the flames,
He danced and stumbled to a piping tune
Played by the headman on a whittled reed.
Two nights he stayed awake to guard the camp
And in the mornings, slept until midday.
On the third day, a wedding party passed –
A caravan, with wagons loaded high
With pomegranates, dates and apricots,
Apples and plums, cherries and nectarines,

Peaches about to burst their ripened skins
Almonds and figs and every type of sweet.
'We're headed east, to Uruk,' one man said,
'And I've been paid to bring the bridal feast.'
'Let's go with them, Shamhat,' said Enkidu
'At least we'll eat and drink along the way.'
So as the party rested, Enkidu
Sat while the barber, carrying out his trade,
Shaved off the wild man's pelt of matted fur,
Massaged his body with sweet-smelling oil
Then washed and combed the hair which, from his head
Flowed down his back in undulating waves.
As Enkidu stood up and faced the sun
A little cloud that hid Shamash's face
Suddenly moved and Shamash, gazing down,
Turned Enkidu into a statue made
Of gold. The barber rubbed his eyes and said
'Like Gilgamesh, this man must be a god.'
'Why do you stare?' asked Enkidu, surprised,
As all the camp, in silence, looked at him.
His beauty for a moment stopped their speech.
Yet far away, under the forest's boughs
A small gazelle still searched for him in vain
And others sniffed the air to catch his scent
But there was nothing carried on the wind
And in his mind no thought of them was left.
So when they walked, next day, into the square
That lay between the temple and the street
Where Uruk's weavers dyed and spun their wool
Into the glorious cloths that made their name,
And people stopped to stare at him and kneel
As he passed by, he laughed and said, 'They seem
To like me here!' Among the wedding guests
The mood grew loud as they approached the house

Where Gilgamesh prepared to have first sex
With the young bride. This troubled Enkidu.
Two at a time, he climbed the marble steps
And shoved away the guardians at the door
Then battered with his fists until the wood
Became a roaring drum to show his rage.
'Gilgamesh, what! Are you an animal?
I've learned from Shamhat how your citizens
Treat one another with respect and care;
Yet now you show your city's darker face
Which makes the feral beasts I've lived with seem
Of higher nature, kinder than yourself!'
The door he pounded slowly opened. Then
Into the light stepped Gilgamesh himself.
Tall as a pillar of the temple, huge
And god-like, this immense colossus
Flung his shadow over Enkidu,
Grabbed the door and hurled it from its hinge;
Then like two bulls set loose, or massive bears
Reared up against each other, or a pair
Of deep-sea monsters whose collision rocks
The earth's foundation to its very core,
They fought. They had no weapons but their own
Bodies, each a hard, unyielding cage
Of muscle, iron bands that smashed together
With such power the lintel cracked and buckled,
Pigeons nesting in the crevices
Of brick flew upwards in a clattering flock
And in the crowd babies began to wail
In terror as their mothers hurried them
Away. First Gilgamesh then Enkidu
Seemed to be winning. Each one had the strength
Of fifty soldiers in the peak of fitness.
As they wrestled on the ground their veins

Stood out like drainpipes on a ziggurat,
Their sinews bulged to bursting and the sweat
Ran down their skin and made clay with the dust.
After two hours, Gilgamesh knelt and said
To Enkidu, 'Wild man, you are the first
That's ever been my equal in a fight.'
He took Enkidu's hand and raised him up
Then held him in his arms. The two men stood
Embracing as if made of marble like
Some carving on a palace wall that seems
So lifelike it could walk away and leave
An empty shape, a story to be told
That changes with the teller and the telling.
Gilgamesh said, 'I saw you first in dreams...'
'A rock and axe, I think,' Enkidu smiled,
'Shamhat has told me.' Then, as if no other
Words were worthy of their breath, they walked
Together, wordless, hand in hand towards
The palace where the goddess Ninsun waited
To receive them. 'You have come at last,'
She said to Enkidu, 'My flesh and blood.
Although you didn't come from my own womb
I love you like a mother loves a son;
You'll be brother for my Gilgamesh.
You'll be a rock to keep him safe, an axe
To guard him and to also set him free.
You'll love him more than life itself and be
A faithful servant to him 'til you die.'
On his hand she put a jasper ring
And round his neck a medal made of gold.
Lord of Wild Places he had been before
And now, the friend of Gilgamesh, whose name
Would carry on forever with his own.

Soon the friends began to make new plans
Daring deeds, adventures still to come
'We'll travel to the forest, find and kill
The giant who guards it, bring back cedar wood
To shore up Uruk's wall,' Gilgamesh said.
The forest shifted on its bed and sighed.
It flickered in Enkidu's mind as if
It brushed up close. He said, 'I knew him when
I roamed the uplands – Humbaba, his speech
Is fire, his breath is death! Enlil has put
Him there to guard the cedars of the gods!
He hears each leaf detach itself and fall
And every raindrop tremble on its twig
And every fawn open its new-born eyes
Across the sixty leagues of wilderness.
A journey there would be our certain end.'
The eyes of Gilgamesh grew hard as stone.
He would have killed a lesser man who had
The courage to defy his will. 'Weakling!'
He said, 'Your spineless words make me despair!
Aren't you the one that lions feared and wolves
Obeyed? Where is your backbone? Have you none?'
'Humbaba, his speech is fire, his breath
Is death!' repeated Enkidu. 'If we
So much as put a toe inside his home
We'll be dead men, or even worse, still living
But afflicted with such agues and shakes
And tremors of the heads and hands, it would
Be better if we'd died!' But Gilgamesh
Was fixed in purpose. To the elders' court
He now dragged Enkidu to put their case.
They heard, 'His speech is fire, his breath is death!'
From Enkidu and shuddered at the risks
Their young and reckless king proposed to take.

But there was nothing that could change his mind;
And Enkidu knew then, whatever fate
Waited for Gilgamesh would also be
His own; and vowing to protect his lord,
Enkidu, in that moment pledged his life
And swore obedience to Gilgamesh.

5

The Goddess Ninsun Prays to the Sun God, Shamash

Gilgamesh asks his mother, the goddess Ninsun, for her blessing on their plans and, knowing she can't deter them, Ninsun begs Shamash to protect them.

His mind resolved | his purpose fixed
But Lady Ninsun | fought his fervor
Flung these fearful | words at Shamash:
'Why have you made | my son so restless?'

Seven times she went | into the sanctum
Seven times crossed | the sacred threshold
Seven times smoothed | herself with oils
With myrrh and | cleansing bergamot.

Then she put on | a clinging dress
Hung precious pendants | round her breasts
Heightened herself | with a high headdress
Crowned with gems | she outshone Aya.

She outshone | the sun's own bride
She lit up | the dawn's first rays.
Her harlots bowed | themselves in awe
Before this lady | charged with light.

Step by step | she climbed the stair
Approached the shrine | of sun god Shamash
As she walked | her censer swung
Sweet-smelling incense | pearled the air.

'Oh Shamash –
when you open the gates of morning for the herds to stream out,
and barley and wheat awake in the earth...

Oh Shamash –
when your touch glistens the fur of wild animals,
and princes of the sky and underworld bow down to you…

Keep your burning eye on Gilgamesh and Enkidu

On the way to the cedar forest make the long road short
On the way to the cedar forest make the short day long
On the way to the cedar forest

Keep your burning eye on Gilgamesh and Enkidu

Command the moon | to guard them at night.
Summon the stars | to stand as sentries
And when you wake | at the first light
Let Aya remind you | to harness the winds.

South wind, north wind | east wind, west
The counterblasts | and tornadoes
The scorching winds | the freezing winds
The storms and gales | and hurricanes.

Let them batter | bold Humbaba
From each side | their forces hurl
Hold him rigid | helpless; then
Let Gilgamesh | deal him his death.

Through your sacred fire
Through myrrh's embers
Grant my desire! Hear me!
Oh Shamash, grant my desire.'

Ninsun's prayer to the sun god Shamash
Jenny Lewis
Oh Sha - mash, when you
o - pen the gates of mor - ning for the herds to stream out, and
bar - ley and wheat a - wake in the earth. Oh
Sha - mash, when your touch glis - tens the fur of wild an - i - mals, and
prin - ces of the sky and un - der - world bow down to you. Keep your bur - ning eye on
Gil - ga - mesh and En - ki - du. On the way to the ce - dar for - est
make the long road short On the way to the ce - dar for - est
make the short day long On the way to the ced - ar for - est
keep your burn - ing eye On Gil - ga - mesh and En - ki - du.

6

Journey to the Cedar Forest

Gilgamesh and Enkidu set off for the Cedar Forest. On the way, they build dream tents so Gilgamesh can receive signs and messages.

Giants, they strode over the land.
After seventy miles they stopped to eat.
After seventy more they camped for the night.
After seventy more they dug a well.
Gilgamesh climbed the mountain peak,
made offerings of barley and wheat.
As the seeds flew on the wind,
birds lifted them, carried his prayers.

Then Enkidu made Gilgamesh
a branchy tent of animal hides,
a door of twigs to keep out rain
and warm inside, a bed of moss.
'Wait for him,' said Enkidu
'Wait for Zaqar, god of dreams.
He brings signals from the moon.
He brings signs from far away.'
Across the doorway down he lay
a net against the watchful world.
Gilgamesh rested until sleep
spilled over him a heavy cloak.

When the moon was at its height,
Gilgamesh woke up stiff with fear:
'The god has turned my blood to ice!
Zaqar has sent me my first dream.
You and I were on a plain
when a mountain fell on us.

As we died our breath was frost,
        our ghosts became the falling snow.'

'My friend, fear not,' said Enkidu,
        'Your dream is good and means all's well.
The worse the dream the better for us,
        for this is Zaqar's secret sign.
The mountain you saw isn't Humbaba,
        it comes from us, it's our own strength.
We'll strike him down and leave him dead,
        for lions and bears to tear apart.'

So up they got and on they went.
        After seventy miles they stopped to eat.
After seventy more they camped for the night.
        After seventy more they dug a well.
Gilgamesh climbed the mountain peak,
        made offerings of barley and wheat.
As the seeds flew on the wind,
        birds lifted them, carried his prayers.

Then Enkidu made Gilgamesh
        a branchy tent of animal hides,
a door of twigs to keep out rain
        and warm inside, a bed of moss.
'Wait for him,' said Enkidu
        'Wait for Zaqar, god of dreams.
He brings signals from the moon.
        He brings signs from far away.'
Across the doorway down he lay
        a net against the watchful world.
Gilgamesh rested until sleep
        spilled over him a heavy cloak.

When the moon was at its height,
            Gilgamesh woke up stiff with fear.
'The god has turned my blood to ice,
            Zaqar has sent my second dream.
This time the mountain threw me down,
            trapped my feet, I couldn't move.
Then out of shining bands of light,
            a man appeared and set me free.'

'My friend, fear not.' said Enkidu,
            'Your dream is good and means all's well.
The worse the dream the better for us,
            for this is Zaqar's secret sign.
The mountain you saw isn't Humbaba,
            it comes from us, it's our own strength.
We'll strike him down and leave him dead,
            for lions and bears to tear apart.'

So up they got and on they went.
            After seventy miles they stopped to eat.
After seventy more they camped for the night.
            After seventy more they dug a well.
Gilgamesh climbed the mountain peak,
            made offerings of barley and wheat.
As the seeds flew on the wind,
            birds lifted them, carried his prayers.

Then Enkidu made Gilgamesh
            a branchy tent of animal hides,
a door of twigs to keep out rain
            and warm inside, a bed of moss.
'Wait for him,' said Enkidu
            'Wait for Zaqar, god of dreams.

He brings signals from the moon.
        He brings signs from far away.'
Across the doorway down he lay
        a net against the watchful world.
Gilgamesh rested until sleep
        spilled over him a heavy cloak.

When the moon was at its height,
        Gilgamesh woke up stiff with fear.
'The god has turned my blood to ice,
        Zaqar has sent me my third dream.
The sky cracked open, the earth quaked,
        lightning flashed and fires broke out,
flames roared up and ash rained down,
        that scorched the land for miles around.'

'My friend, fear not.' said Enkidu,
        'Your dream is good and means all's well.
The worse the dream the better for us,
        for this is Zaqar's secret sign.
The fires you saw, the lightning flash,
        were flames around the giant Humbaba.
We'll strike him down and leave him dead
        for lions and bears to tear apart.'

So up they got and on they went.
        After seventy miles they stopped to eat.
After seventy more they camped for the night.
        After seventy more they dug a well.
Gilgamesh climbed the mountain peak,
        made offerings of barley and wheat.
As the seeds flew on the wind,
        birds lifted them, carried his prayers.

Then Enkidu made Gilgamesh
            a branchy tent of animal hides,
a door of twigs to keep out rain
            and warm inside, a bed of moss.
'Wait for him,' said Enkidu
            'Wait for Zaqar, god of dreams.
He brings signals from the moon.
He brings signs from far away.'
            Across the doorway down he lay
a net against the watchful world.
            Gilgamesh rested until sleep
spilled over him a heavy cloak.

When the moon was at its height,
            Gilgamesh woke up stiff with fear.
'The god has turned my blood to ice,
            Zaqar has sent me my fourth dream.
It's worse than all the other dreams!
            A Thunderbird was hovering high,
it rose above us in a cloud,
            its face was blackened, breathing fire.
Then a man came, quiet and calm
            bound its wings and threw it down.
On its neck he placed his boot,
            then stamped on it until it died!'

'My friend, fear not,' said Enkidu,
            'Your dream is good and means all's well.
The worse the dream the better for us,
            for this is Zaqar's secret sign.
The Thunderbird is your own fear,
            your own fear of giant Humbaba.
Shamash will come to give us strength.
            With his help we'll kill that thug!'

So up they got and on they went.
    After seventy miles they stopped to eat.
After seventy more they camped for the night.
    After seventy more they dug a well.
Gilgamesh climbed the mountain peak,
    made offerings of barley and wheat.
As the seeds flew on the wind,
    birds lifted them, carried his prayers.

Then Enkidu made Gilgamesh
    a branchy tent of animal hides,
a door of twigs to keep out rain
    and warm inside, a bed of moss.
'Wait for him,' said Enkidu
    'Wait for Zaqar, god of dreams.
He brings signals from the moon.
    He brings signs from far away.'
Across the doorway down he lay
    a net against the watchful world.
Gilgamesh rested until sleep
    spilled over him a heavy cloak.

When the moon was at its height,
    Gilgamesh woke up stiff with fear.
'The god has turned my blood to ice,
    Zaqar has sent me my fifth dream.
I was clinging to a bull
    that bellowed as it tore the ground.
A tower of dust came from its hooves.
    I shouted as it threw me down.
A man appeared and caught me safe,
    then from my face he wiped the blood,
he placed his arm beneath my head,
    he gave me water, let me rest.'

'My friend, fear not,' said Enkidu,
        'Your dream is good and means all's well.
The worse the dream, the better for us,
        for this is Zaqar's secret sign.
The wild bull was sun god Shamash.
        He will lift us out of danger;
His fiery sword will scorch the ground.
        The man who came to give you water
was none other than your father.
        This dream means we'll make our names!
Be legends 'til the end of time!'

7

The Battle with Humbaba

The friends reach the cedar forest and enter it, preparing to fight the giant Humbaba, appointed by the deities as its guardian.

Broken-sandalled, thirsty from the road,
out of the sun's fierce stare into this mass
of shifting spars

shifting light
like
broken stars

fluting, piping, swelling, fading,
barefoot, underfoot, hooved and horned
every stem filled up with juice

sounds
of life shimmering
stammering

banks of shade cajole the eye,
bark and leaf mould, spotted
and barred, green and anchored, anchored
and bowed
a tethered, splendid mass of billowing

cool
flickering
shifting light

this patched, striped and furred world,
this feathered, fecund cradle of wingbeats,
this paradise, song, hymn to the goddess
this womb, this holy, pregnant gourd

they penetrate with unsheathed sword

while

axes bite the trunks of cedars

cedars groan as axes bite

the people of Girsu are shaken by tremors

the babies of Uruk are woken by thunder

cracked and sharp the cries of cedars

the giant hunkers

silent, listening

the forest whispers

back, go back,
Humbaba's blood
is thick and black
his speech is fire
his breath is death
a cedar branch
shall be your wreath.

sheets of sweat from the king's brow; terror floods his muscles, his feet take root

the forest murmurs

back, go back,
Humbaba's blood
is thick and black

then they see him, his mile-long
shadow slips over them like smoke
round his waist a skirt of corpses,
round his neck a chain of skulls.

Like a ziggurat so tall it blocks the sun
Like tree root clubs his massive hands
Like flying blood his radiant auras

[GILGAMESH TO ENKIDU] *'Let's go back...'*

Like cadavers risen from the ground his stink
Like entrails of a bull his face as if slaughtered
Like roars of under-ocean pebbles his voice

[HUMBABA to GILGAMESH] *'Sir, I'm pleased to*
meet you. Please do
me the honour of
respecting my
forest!'

[GILGAMESH to ENKIDU] *'Enkidu, let's go back'*

[ENKIDU to GILGAMESH] *'Have you no*
backbone, are you
spineless?'

[HUMBABA to ENKIDU] *'You'll soon be*
spineless too, you
motherless,
fatherless, ungrateful
son of a tadpole!
Didn't I give you the

freedom of my forest
to run wild in with
your gazelles?'

[GILGAMESH to ENKIDU] *'LET'S GO BACK!'*

[ENKIDU to GILGAMESH] *'It's too late!'*

As if a mountain had blown itself open.
As if burning flesh was raining down
and stinking gobbets fell around them

Humbaba belches out the stench of death –
reaches his huge hand towards Enkidu

[GILGAMESH, SHOUTING] *'SHAMASH! Help us!'*

while

in far-off Uruk the goddess Ninsun
swings her censer

the scent of myrrh drifts up to
Shamash

Shamash calls his warrior winds

As if from the horizon a thousand fighters.
As if a thousand devils wailing, the
shrieking north wind, armoured and
helmeted, stops Humbaba in his tracks.

He can't go forwards.

As if from the depths a thousand bulls.
As if a thousand demons screaming, the
roaring south wind, hooved and
horned, traps Humbaba with its force.

He can't go back.

Now he tries to slip to the side, but
from the east and west, the whirlwinds
gather and spin, freezing, scorching
typhoons and tempests. Trees fly
in flocks. Animals twist and turn in the
streaming currents. The river is snatched
from its bed and floats like a ribbon above
the forest.

He can't go sideways.

Humbaba's voice comes through the hubbub…

[HUMBABA] *'Spare me,*
Gilgamesh!'

[ENKIDU to GILGAMESH] *'We have to kill him!'*

[HUMBABA] *'Take what you want*
but let me live,

Gilgamesh! Two-thirds god and one-third king… I will serve you faithfully.'

[GILGAMESH] *'Let's spare him! We can take what timber we need.'*

[ENKIDU] *'We can't trust him! Strike him! Strike!'*

He's chained by the winds, but his eyes move, pleading. Up the heroes climb and up and up as if up terraces stretching to the sky they climb his rigid body. Then with their swords and axes go to work, hacking through veins and sinews 'til tough skin splits, the neck starts to sever, creaks, cracks. The huge head lolls for a moment as if listening to whispers, then drops to earth with a mountainous crash.

while

the forest screams, and
then falls silent

on Mount Cedar, the deities
stop to listen

Gilgamesh and Enkidu fell
the cedars

the gods and goddesses
look down in horror

Slipping out of the forest, sliding out from under the canopy, dirt covered.

cooling, stiffening
world gone cold

On the bright river their bodies shine. The raft of lashed cedars takes an hour to walk down, its figurehead, the head of Humbaba, huge and solid, skin like tree bark, hair a tangle of creepers from which the last birds leave. Slowly the wooden snake moves into the wide straits beyond the forest, its prow barely ripples the water. Smaller it gets and smaller, until it's just a smudge on the horizon wiped off by a thumb

while

tears

the forest floor
is leaking blood

fall

Shamash shrugs.
The die is cast…

down

forest
shrouds
clouds

pale
austere
spare

aghast with scars

like

broken

stars

8

Inanna and Gilgamesh

Gilgamesh and Enkidu return to Uruk in triumph.
After bathing and dressing in clean clothes, Gilgamesh appears on the palace balcony to greet the crowd.

He was built like a door, solid as cedar,
Thighs like a bull's, brazen and bulging.
He washed his hair so it rippled like the Tigris,
Shook it down so it shone like the Euphrates.

His body caught the sun like a muscled river,
Eyes dark as wine at the base of a pitcher.
Crowned with gold he was glorious and godly.
Gilgamesh was glorious and godly.

She took one look, it stopped her breath
As if a fire ran under her skin
As if knocked down by an iron bell
Inanna saw Gilgamesh, and fell.

Goddess of war, thunderbolt-thrower,
She shook with desire like a reed in the reed bed.
Her lungs lost their power, her voice became lower
She opened to Gilgamesh like a small flower –

'Come, love, into my sweet-smelling chamber
In a golden chariot studded with amber
Drawn by a team of lions and mules
With bridles of silver and bolts of blue lapis.

As you cross my threshold my door will caress you,
You'll conquer my court as you conquer my heart.
Our reign will bring bounty, be fertile and fecund
Each goat shall have triplets, each ewe shall have twins.

Our donkeys and horses shall outrace the wind
Our oxen each day shall plough a deep furrow
Our orchards and farmland shall give a full harvest
Our seas with a rich crop of silver be blessed.

Only come to me, Gilgamesh, we shall be wed
Lie close to me on my perfumed bed.'

Gilgamesh turned to look at Inanna.
Looked through his lashes at holy Inanna,
Sneered, 'You! Who would marry you?
You're a dog in the road crawling with fleas.

You're a blade of frost scraping the ice
A broken door that lets the wind through
A cup that cuts the lip of the drinker
A shoe that bites the foot of its owner.

You're a palace that maims its own heroes
A fireplace that puts out its own fire
A fortress that slaughters its own soldiers
An elephant that kills its own mahout.'

As if her guts had turned to whey
Inanna gasped as shock ran through her.
Like a shower of stones his insults hit.
Like enemy troops his words attacked.

Gilgamesh felt his powers grow strong
His two-thirds god surged up inside.
Had he not killed the giant Humbaba?
Now he would humble holy Inanna.

'What became of all your bridegrooms?
Dumuzi, your first, the beautiful youth
You fucked for months in a tangle of sheets
Then you sent him to rot in hell.

The Bright-Speckled Roller Bird, where is he?
Each night he held you to his breast
'Til you clouted him and now from the trees
He cries *my wing, my wing, my wing!*

You tempted Ishallanu, your father's slave
Who used to bring you baskets of dates,
When he ran from you and hid in the reeds
You turned him into a warty toad!'

Inanna's eyes grew cold as slate
Her growl of rage a thunderous belch
The veins of her neck stood out like vines.
She spat words like a hail of spears:

'You! You're only two-thirds god!
I'll strike the part of you that's human.
Your tears will stream like a river in spate,
I'll send a storm to crush your heart!'

Then up she climbed on columns of air
Climbed up to her father's house
On ropes of light she climbed the sky
Like a shooting star she lit up heaven.

After a day she took off her crown
Took off her crown of gold and lapis
Threw it down so she could go faster
So she could go faster than any wind.

After two days she took off her breastplate
Took off her breastplate of bronze and silver
Threw it down so she could go faster
So she could go faster than any wind.

After three days she took off her anklets
Took off her anklets of amber and amethyst
Threw them down so she could go faster
So she could go faster than any wind.

After four days she took off her rings
Took off her rings of turquoise and topaz
Threw them down so she could go faster
So she could go faster than any wind.

After five days she took off her earrings
Took off her earrings of white and black onyx
Threw them down so she could go faster
So she could go faster than any wind.

After six days she took off her girdle
Took off her girdle of jasper and jade
Threw it down so she could go faster
So she could go faster than any wind.

After seven days she took off her bangles
Took off her bangles of pyrite and pearl
Threw them down so she could go faster
So she could go faster than any wind.

Naked, she arrived in heaven
Knelt before her father Anu
Asked him for the heavenly Sky Bull
Swore revenge on Gilgamesh.

With the Sky Bull she'd destroy him
Kill the king, lay waste the land.
Anu said, 'This can't be done
You cannot take the Bull of Heaven.'

'I'll open up the gates of hell!
And wake the dead!' Inanna screamed
'I'll set them free to eat the living
There'll be no soul left on earth!'

Anu knew he could not argue
With his rampant eldest daughter.
The gates of heaven began to tremble
And Anu let her have the Sky Bull.

Inanna called the Heavenly Bull,
Her words flew like a flock of birds.
She called again and it was night
And at her call he came to her.

Inanna led him down from heaven
Where he grazed among the planets,
Round his flanks light danced and spun
And he was made of stars and burning.

His eyes were meteors big as moons
His tail a trail of flaming comets
Each tuft of hair a galaxy
Each breath a moving constellation.

When the Sky Bull's hoof touched down
It smashed to dust the town of Girsu
When its second hoof touched down
It set eight miles of fields ablaze.

When the bull's third hoof touched down
It opened up a nine-mile crater
When the bull's fourth hoof touched down
Ten thousand strong men toppled in.

When he bowed his head to drink
In one great gulp he drained Euphrates
When he raised his tail to piss
The Tigris rose and burst its banks.

'Shamash!' shouted Gilgamesh
'Help us kill the Bull of Heaven!
Guide our spears into his heart
Give each axe a burning edge.'

Shamash saw he had a chance –
A chance to equal great Inanna,
His rays blazed down on Sky Bull's back
And turned to salt its pelt of stars.

Bit by bit the Sky Bull shrank
Like a moon it waned and paled,
One hero grabbed it by its tail
The other grabbed it by its horns.

In its throat Gilgamesh thrust
Through sinewed chink his bitter blade.
The Sky Bull stumbled to its knees –
Its bawling woke the far-off gods.

One by one its stars went out.
One by one its planets dimmed.
One by one its meteors faded.
One by one its comets vanished.

Then Gilgamesh cut out its heart
To give to Shamash their protector.
Enkidu hacked off its haunch
And hurled it in Inanna's face.

Inanna called her prostitutes
Inanna called her courtesans
Together they sang mourning rites
Over the dead Bull of Heaven.

Gilgamesh called his silversmiths
Gilgamesh called his jewellers
Told them to decorate the horns
To hang up on his palace wall.

Festivities went on all night
But later when the palace slept
Enkidu had a chilling dream
The underworld was calling him.

Erishkagel opened one eye –
A moon so cold it froze his blood.
He raised a hand to shield his face
Then she whispered, 'Come to me.'

A rod of ice lay on the bed
Between himself and Gilgamesh.
The gods declared their punishment:

Enkidu must die.

9

The Death of Enkidu

Over twelve nights and days Enkidu sickens and dies.
As his friend's consciousness slips away Gilgamesh is distraught with grief.
Enkidu rages against death and is visited by horrifying visions.

It is almost beyond

... it is almost beyond hearing

light crowns, is born, a delicate shell
a tentative cavity of mesh and strands

he knows

... he knows troops disband
when the leader is lost

now

his last breaths are being counted

'my friend the sun has deserted me!'

sound is a shower of sparks

taste goes, feeling goes

while

he thinks the door is a man *he curses the door made of cedars*
they stole from the forest

they use the same cedars
to fire his coffin kiln

no more skins, the trap is empty *he curses the hunter*

she dreams of thorns and rags *he curses Shamhat*
a soldier empties his guts on her

'oh forest, let me re-enter you!'

sheets of rain from the king's eyes

The lion-eagle/thunder-bringer/man-like-a-wild-bull pins him

'save me, Gilgamesh! It has
turned my arms into wings!'

under the rib's eaves a quiet cavity

his last breaths are being counted

'the dead eat soil and clay!'

'the dead are owls and doves!'

while

his lungs are turning back into forests

he lifts his curse on Shamhat –
(she wakes on a bed of gold and lapis lazuli)

Erishkagel shows him her black teeth

because he did not die in battle

because flesh turns to maggots

the coffin has been fired and decorated

light crowns, is born, a delicate shell

and now he is

'roo-coo, roo-coo'

beyond

hearing

10

Enkidu's Funeral

At the first glimmer of light, Gilgamesh's grief overflows.

Unexpected rain darkens the courtyard.

A slant of crows over the fields.

May the hills and mountains mourn you. May the meadows lament like your mother. Like a young gazelle, trapped by the hunter, like a fawn in the thicket, you laid yourself down. When a maggot fell from your cheekbone, I had to leave your body. O Enkidu, my brother, my brother…

Through a mist the dawn rose.

A hail of gulls over the sea.

In my dream, the warmth of your mouth. May the shepherd mourn you. May the ploughboy mourn you. Like a young wolf… like a lion… I'll lay your body to rest among lilies. Over your face I'll draw a veil. O Enkidu, my brother, my brother...

He called his coppersmiths and his goldsmiths.
He called his silversmiths and his jewellers.
He called his sculptors and his craftsmen
to make a statue of Enkidu that would last forever.

He called his butchers and his bread-makers.
He called his beekeepers and his wine-makers.
He called his yoghourt-makers and his dairy maids
to prepare the funeral feast for Enkidu.

He called his bow-makers and his wood-carvers.
He called his weavers and his cloth-dyers.
He called his lute-makers and his lyre-makers
to prepare the grave gifts for Enkidu.

For the gods and goddesses of the underworld.
For the Annunaki of the underworld.
For the elders and wise-women of the underworld.
For the cleaners and the sweepers of the underworld.

For Bibbu, the butcher, he sent a whetstone of obsidian.
For Quassa-tabat, the cleaner, he sent a silver bracelet.
For Dumuzi, the shepherd, he sent a flute of cornelian
So they would walk by Enkidu's side and be his friends.

For Erishkagel, queen of death, he sent a throne of cedar.
For Inanna, queen of life, he sent a cloth of gold.
For Shamash, the sun god, he sent a golden lyre
So they would walk by Enkidu's side and be his friends.

Then Gilgamesh looked on Enkidu's face for the last time.

O my brother, my brother… O Enkidu. I'll lay your body to rest among lilies…

A hail of gulls over the sea.

Through a mist, the dawn rose.

Like a fawn in the thicket, you laid yourself down. May the hills and mountains mourn you...may the meadows lament like your mother…

A slant of crows over the fields.

Unexpected rain darkens the courtyard.

11

Gilgamesh in the Wilderness

Grieving for Enkidu, Gilgamesh wanders in the wilderness.
He reveals to Shamash his own fear of death.

Rough with regret | far from home
The heft of his heart | a heavy burden
Gored by grief | wretched with woe
Sorrow knotted | the cords of his neck.

Gilgamesh cried | not just for Enkidu.
Cried for himself | for having to follow
Follow his friend | into the underworld
Never again | see the light of the sun.

Blind in darkness | he could not be
So he searched | for Uta-napishtim
Uta-napishtim | the sun of souls
The one who Ea | saved from the Flood.

All around him | lions were watching
Their topaz eyes | shone like shields
Once, then twice | he swung his axe
The lions fell | gave up their lives.

He ate their flesh | wore their skins.
Grew bony and gaunt | lost his strength
Slept only little | waited for dawn
To feast his eyes | on Shamash's fire.

'O SHAMASH, *as you close the gates of evening when the herds are safely in*
... where does your light go?

O SHAMASH, *when the moon casts wing-shadows and bats flit silent*
over the earth
... how much light is left?

O SHAMASH, *when I follow my friend into the underworld*
... will you desert me?

O SHAMASH, *when I follow Enkidu into the darkness*
... will I never see your light again?'

Shamash asked | 'What are you seeking?
Only the gods | can live forever
Only the gods | escape from death
For men and women | life must end.'

So Gilgamesh | went on his way
Came at last | to Mashu Mountain
Rising from | the deepest sea bed
To the highest | arch of heaven.

In the mountain's | pleasant shade
Pearled with dew | until the dawn
There it is | that Shamash sleeps
At the end | of each day's turn.

And rearing up | into the clouds
That clothe the foothills | of the mountain
A scorpion man | and scorpion woman
Guard the gates | let no-one pass.

On each head | six pairs of eyes
Glitter sharply | ever watchful
On each back | a metal coat
A carapace | catches the sun.

Six legs each has | to run at speed
Or scuttle into | monstrous lairs
And mighty pincers | poised to grab
And delve into | their wretched prey.

Worst of all | the bulbous stingers
Each one tipped | with deadly poison
Wave above | each creature's head
Curved and lethal | poised to strike.

When Gilgamesh | caught sight of them
At first he couldn't | make them out
Through the cloud | a claw-shaped crag?
A bronze plateau? | A glittering peak?

With a jolt | of disbelief
He recognised | the hideous brutes
As scorpions | of foul nightmares
That must be put there | by the gods.

He staggered sideways | reeled back
Thought his final | hour had come
But as he cowered | a deafening roar –
The buzzing talk | of scorpions.

'He's a god' | said scorpion-man
'But one third man' | said scorpion-woman
'He must have | the gods' protection
So we shouldn't | cause him harm.'

'Where are you from?' | asked scorpion-man
'I'm Gilgamesh | king of Uruk.'
'Where are you going?' | asked scorpion-woman
'I'm searching for | Uta-napishtim

To ask him for | eternal life
That's my task | from which I can
By nobody | be turned aside.'
Gilgamesh stood | and bowed his head

Prepared for death | or any fate
The scorpion-beings | could inflict.
The buzzing noise | again grew strong
The sound of scorpion | consultation.

'We know the way' | said scorpion-man
'But none can win' | said scorpion-woman.
'You must run | through Machu mountain
Twelve by twelve hours | no-one can do it.

Before sunrise | you must get through
Or you'll meet death | in that dark tomb.'
Gilgamesh thought | 'It's the only way,'
And ran at once | into the cave.

He ran six hours | it was black as coal
He ran six more | it was black as pitch
He ran six more | it was black as soot
He ran six more | it was black as night

The black was black | as the blackest of cats
The black was black | as a pack of black rats
Two seconds left | to finish the race
The tunnel's mouth | a shimmering haze

Just in time | he reached the end
Burst from blindness | into brilliance
Found himself | in the gods' garden
A grove of gold | glittering with gems.

Carnelian trees | with glowing grapes
Cherries of coral | raspberries of ruby
Apples of amethyst | amber apricots
Pears of peridot | peaches of pearl.

Dazed by dazzle | Gilgamesh gasped
He gazed around | the glorious garden
Flowers flourished | filled with fragrance
He breathed in | their sweet aromas.

And far away | a woman waited
Sacred Siduri | silent and shrouded
Keeping secrets | of the gods
Even at the edge | of the world.

12

Gilgamesh at the Edge of the World

Gilgamesh leaves the Garden of Jewels and struggles on in his quest to find Uta-napishtim, the Flood survivor. He reaches the edge of the world where he comes across a tavern kept by the demi-goddess, Siduri.

Shrouded in hoods and veils she lived alone
At the sea's edge beside the salty spray
And she was tough as wind-blown marram grass
Whose roots creep craftily beneath the dunes
And bind themselves to knot the flying sand.
Her dishes, racks and cups were solid gold
Her wine and beer was casked and kept in gold
Her tavern only visited by gods.
She saw him coming from a long way off
At first a speck, a spot, a moving dot
But closer up she saw he was a man
So trouble-scarred, a leather sheath of bones
His face a pitted shield of dents and hacks
That life had dealt him, or the stony world.
As he drew near she ran to bolt her gate
With shackled breath, her chest a tightened strap
Of terror as she climbed up on her roof.
'You! Woman! Open up!' His shout was rough
She gave back words to him in eme-sal
'First tell me who you are and why you're here
And why you batter rudely at my door?'
With this soft speech she tamed his seething wrath
He dragged his fingers through his matted hair
And writhing in his woe he told his tale.
When she had heard it she held out her hand
And led him to her table straight away
And sat him down and gave him beer and bread
And spoke to him as she would any king.
'The path you've come is far yet it must stop

As every other's must except the gods'
Deep in the earth's loamed bed where you will sleep
And tread the dream-road to its bitter end.'
At this the listener's tears began to stream
Like hares across a field in wintry sun.
Siduri spoke once more and took his hand
'Your wife and children wait for you at home
Be wise! Go back again to Uruk's fold –
Among your kindred you'll find warmth of heart
Is worth more than a thousand precious rings –
And love, not battle glory, is life's gift.'

Yet Gilgamesh's mind would not be still
His thoughts, already striding back and forth
Were restless as a wolf who's lost her young
And he harped on again about his need
To find the one who overcame the Flood,
Uta-napishtim in his island den.
Siduri saw this hunger like a bone
He'd gnaw on as if starving with no rest
So, winding on her shrouds against the wind
She showed him to a clearing in the woods
Where boatman Ur-shanabi patched his nets
Then she was gone and him left to his luck.

To his request the boatman shook his head.
He said the journey was too dangerous.
Then with a torrent thundering in his blood
Rage gripped the heart of thwarted Gilgamesh
'How dare you speak like this against your king!
Do you not see that I am two-thirds god?
In Uruk this would surely mean your death.'
And with a stream of oaths, he swung his axe
Until the heavy blocks the boatman used

To navigate lay smashed, and there was nothing
Left to steer his boat across the sea.
So Gilgamesh's purpose had been wrecked
Once more by actions of his willful self.
Now Ur-shanabi sent him to the woods
To find the strongest trees for punting poles.
Exactly fifty feet each pole must be
Straight as the level spear-shaft as it flies
And each must have a bole of equal girth
And each be buffed, and finished with a boss.
At last they had three hundred stowed away
And it was time to board the boatman's craft.
Three days it took to reach the Sea of Death
When usually it took more than a month
So vigorously the boat had flashed along
At dolphin-speed with Gilgamesh to steer.
Now Ur-shanabi urged him to slow down
For if a drop of water touched them, they
Would wither instantly and turn to stone
and to the bottom of the Sea of Death
they'd sink together, never to return.
Gilgamesh then took up the punting poles
And one by one, he drove them to the depths
And when he had none left, they found they'd crossed
The Sea of Death; yet there were miles to go
Before they reached the archipelago
On which Uta-napishtim and his wife
Had spent the woeful years since the great Flood.
So Gilgamesh stood up and spread his arms
To make his shirt a sail to catch the wind.
He was himself the rigging and the spar
That steered them to the Flood survivor's home.

13

Uta-Napishtim the Flood Survivor

Gilgamesh meets Uta-napishtim and his wife and begs for the secret of immortality.

Although their eyes had now begun to fail
they still could glimpse across the bulging sea
a mast with ragged tunic for a sail

and recognised the boat of Ur-shanabi.
Against the cries of seagulls and the crash
of waves they hurried down towards the quay

where they got their first sight of Gilgamesh
a shabby figure made of skin and bone
with hollow cheeks and slackened, sunburned flesh

from whom all spark of youth and health seemed gone.
'Do you not know me?' this strange sailor said,
'I'm Gilgamesh who sits upon the throne

of far off Uruk where the date palms shade
a glorious city circled by a wall
of sun-fired bricks that my own subjects made.'

Uta-napishtim countered with a smile
'And this is how a king looks, nowadays?
Have ceremonial robes gone out of style?'

Gilgamesh knelt down on the ground and gave
a long and sobbing sigh which filled the air
and brought with it a murmur from the grave

a shudder from the world below them where
old Belet-seri kept accounts of all
the feathered souls who lived in darkness there.

Now it was time for Gilgamesh to tell
Uta-napishtim and his wife the tale
of Enkidu and how pride took its toll

when they as heroes went beyond the pale
and killed Humbaba in his sacred place
and hacked to death Inanna's great Sky Bull;

how punishment was swift and merciless
and Enkidu's slow death a pall of grief
that blinds the inner eye of Gilgamesh.

'I beg you for the gift of endless life
the gift that you have, granted by the gods:
I'm two-thirds god. It must be mine by right?'

Uta-napisthim heard these pleading words
and pitied Gilgamesh his dismal mood.
He said, 'The gift of life was my reward

because when Enlil sent the mighty Flood
Ea came to me one night to warn me first
to make a vessel, huge, of cedar wood

then gather seed of all that came from earth
each plant and bush, each tree, each bird that flies
each creature that is able to give birth

and bring them to the ark for sanctuary.
I toiled to finish well before the storm
so when the tempest howled across the sky

and people cried as they began to drown,
the river rose to swallow all in sight
except my craft which floated, light as down.

Even the gods and goddesses took fright
and lay curled on the ground in sheeting rain
as dogs crouched by a wall in terror might

who, trembling, wait for rescue, but in vain.
The sea became a city of the dead
and fishes made the forests their terrain

each cedar branch with moonstone scales inlaid
each date palm grove a giant bed for whales
each mountain peak a rock beneath the waves.

Six days and nights the violent typhoon raged
then on the seventh, all was motionless
the warrior winds of Shamash had been caged.

At dawn, a dazzling brightness met my eyes –
I flung the window open and then gazed
in awe upon a mirrored paradise.

Near to Mount Nimrush now we castaways
waited for sinking waters to reveal
the slopes of mountains or some solid place

where we could disembark our crew of souls.
A dove flew out but then returned again
a swallow also flew back to the fold

but when I set the raven free it went
bobbing and bowing on its patch of land
finding once more its source of nourishment.

As the waters drained away we found
no humans left on earth except for us.
We had escaped the fate Enlil had planned.

So Aruru gave us this new status –
alone of humankind to be immortal –
and how we long for this to be reversed:

to be allowed to pass through that same portal
that you so dread, my friend, that you so dread;
who wants eternal life when flesh is frail?

But tell me, Gilgamesh, are you prepared
to see if death can really test your mettle?
First try defeating sleep, you'll find it hard

but if you can survive this easier battle
there may be hope that death can be outrun.'
So Gilgamesh, to see if he was able

to face this feat, knelt where the lash of brine
kept him awake; and sleep at first was banished –
until the evening when a fog came down

to cover him; and then his eyelids drooped
and sleep surged through him in a sudden wave.
Uta-napishtim's wife baked loaves of bread

and placed them in a row to mark the days
since Gilgamesh had lost himself in sleep.
When he, the dreamer, woke, he was amazed

and knew that he could not withstand the breach
through which death hooks us down; for all his royal
state, this demi-god himself beneath

death's cloak of dust would sink and into total
darkness fade from view and memory –
his precious life and all its moments spoiled.

'King Gilgamesh, you must try to enjoy
the life you have as it will not last long'
Uta-napishtim counselled him, 'your story

will be set down and your great name belong
to history, and people will relate
your deeds at festivals in dance and song.

And Ur-shanabi, also, from this date
will be remembered down the centuries
because he had the chance to navigate

the boat that brought the godly king to me.'
Before they left, Uta-napishtim's wife,
wanting to show Gilgamesh sympathy,

told where a plant that couldn't give him life
but could renew his youth for years to come
grew on the seabed; so into the surf

Gilgamesh plunged and battling through the spume
to where the plant was growing on a reef
he took his knife and cut it from its home;

then, shooting upwards on a long-held breath
he held it in the air triumphantly
and laughed with Ur-shanabi as they both

clambered aboard the raft and cast away
with shouts of thanks and soon were riding high
again above the ever-bounding waves.

14

The Plant of Youth

Gilgamesh and Ur-shanabi make their way home to Uruk with the Plant of Youth.

The heat like molten glass cascaded down
With pins of fire inside each grain of sand
That scorched their feet; but still they stumbled on
Two puny figures in a ruthless land
When all at once in the far distance shone
What seemed to them to be a jewelled band
A bracelet or an ornate silver wreath
Dropped on the highway by a casual thief.

They walked towards it, thinking it might fade
And disappear, a mirage in the smooth
Expanses of the desert, yet it stayed –
A lake set like a gemstone in its grove.
In they both plunged, and soon began to wade
Deeper, then swam down where rushes wove
Among the weeds, meshes of light and shade
As on the surface, date palm shadows played:

After a while, they stumbled to the bank
Their bodies cool and burnished by the light
And on a patch of springy grass, they sank
Down to rest, watching the darting flight
Of dragonflies that came to flit and drink
And hover on the water, exquisite.
As Gilgamesh was drowsing, close to sleep
He caught a sudden movement on the slope –

A snake, dun-coloured, made towards the plant
He'd left abandoned at the waterside

When he and Ur-shanabi had, imprudent,
Dived straight in, and now at gathering speed
It skimmed across the sand in silence, bent
On stealing magic for itself, and opened wide
Its jaws and swallowed it. Now no lament
On heaven or earth could properly express
The anguish felt by careless Gilgamesh.

As its old skin was sloughed, the canny snake
Emerged new-born with radiant symmetries
Of golds and greens of every subtle shade –
A moving rainbow, dazzling to the eyes.
How Gilgamesh's heart began to ache
When he saw how, with this same alchemy
He could have been reborn, again made young
A newly sharpened axe, a harp restrung.

And now it seemed that life could get no worse.
For all his hopes and plans it was too late.
Failure pursued him, constant as a curse.
Only old age and death still lay in wait.
The loan of life must soon be reimbursed.
And even he could not escape this fate.
And even he could not turn back the tide.
And even he, part god, could not survive.

His youthful recklessness came back to him.
The memory of how he'd tried to force
His people into slavery; his aim
Above all else, to change the natural course
Of history, trade everything for fame –
Now filled his heart with anguish and remorse.
Faced again with the mistakes he'd made
He shuddered as they stabbed him like a blade.

Night fell, and he knelt, motionless, beneath
A sky embroidered by a net of stars
And made no sound, so heavy was his grief
It made a wound in him too deep for tears.
He understood at last that life is brief,
Each moment to be grasped as it appears
And lived with gratitude, not thrown away
As he had done with pride and vanity.

He was a granite shadow, stiff and still
Except the knotted sinews of his neck
Which showed he battled with the gidim xul –
Ghosts of the past that filled him with regret
That they had killed Inanna's heavenly bull,
Insulted her and shown her no respect.
This was the cause of the worst hurt he knew:
The loss of his beloved Enkidu.

The gods looked down and pitied Gilgamesh.
They thought it time to take away his pain.
Now he was asking their forgiveness
They answered with a shower of healing rain
That cleansed his heart so he could start afresh
Turn mourning into morning once again.
So he and Ur-shanabi travelled on
And Gilgamesh's tale is almost done.

15

Homecoming

Gilgamesh returns to Uruk.

At sunset now | the wall is gold
Cast from light | are Uruk's bricks.
'Come with me' | says Gilgamesh
To Ur-shanabi | 'Come with me'.

Up they climb | a hundred steps
And up again | a hundred more
Along the wall | they start to walk
Around Uruk | together tread.

Outside the gates | the desert sprawls
Shamash is king | with crown of fire.
Across the sky | the eagle skims
Across the dunes | the wind, the wind.

Inside, Inanna's | temple tall
Over the city | throws its shade
Shadow fingers | creeping out
Towards the river | great Euphrates.

Creeping slowly | spreading far
Past Eanna's | hanging gardens
Like a rich | embroidery
Each pomegranate | each fresh flower.

Outside the wall | an empty waste.
Outside, a vulture's | silent flight.
Inside the wall | a bright brocade.
Inside, the thrum | and throng of life.

Ur-shanabi | laughs and says
'Of this you are | the architect!
From your own mind | this paradise
This human feat | this precious gem.

'Across the world | you will be praised
Across the world | forever known
O Gilgamesh | your fame will live
Your glory sung | until the end.'

Epilogue

surpassing all kings
his name is a legend
his people kept safe
in the sheepfold of Uruk
unmatched in combat
none could defeat him
mighty and handsome
a glorious hero

the full womb
the still grave
the weight of life
heavy as a flood
how the waters broke
how the world was birthed –
Gilgamesh knew.
He understood.

Afterword

Because the origins of the *Epic of Gilgamesh* lie in an oral tradition it has always been an innately unstable text, open to unlimited creative responses. These include poetry, prose, visual art, operas (including *The Epic of Gilgamesh* by the Czech composer, Bohuslav Martinů, 1955), ballets (including *Gilgamesh and Enkidu* by the Russian-born French composer, Alexandre Danilovski, arranged for 'orchestra and wolves' voices', 2012); TV series (including *Gilgamesh*, 2003–2004, a twenty-six-part animation series set in a future where the sky has been changed into a giant mirror); films and video games. When approaching my own version, I decided to follow the advice of Vera Schneider in her philosophical study *Gilgamesh* (1967), in which she argues that we must attempt a 'spiritual-intellectual re-orientation' so that we can return to an 'intuitive grasp' in order to engage with the epic at a subliminal level rather than treat it with too much reverence as a historical artefact – although both its history and provenance are fascinating in themselves. Predating Homer by at least 1,500 years, the *Epic of Gilgamesh* was discovered by mid-Victorian archaeologists excavating the ruined library of the Assyrian King Ashurbanipal (circa 650 BC). Written in cuneiform on hundreds of often broken and damaged clay tablets, the epic tells the story of a powerful leader who abuses his power and whose hubris leads to punishment by the gods. Some of the themes are startlingly relevant today.

Gilgamesh was an actual king who ruled over the city of Uruk sometime between 2,700–2,600 BC and stories about him must have been circulating soon after his death which were developed with pre-existent material throughout the Sumerian era. These early versions were subsequently translated into and developed in Akkadian. Sumerian is a language unrelated to any other language. Akkadian is a Semitic language, as are the later languages of Aramaic, Hebrew and Arabic. There were Assyrian and Babylonian dialects of Akkadian, both spoken and written.

In the Akkadian manifestation of the *Gilgamesh* epic we can already see changes to the narrative, and the introduction of new prosodic or textual effects, perhaps as a way of updating the piece for performance at the court or temple, but, also, to enable it to chime with different mores and appeal to a new, contemporary audience. Samuel Noah Kramer, in *History Begins at Sumer*, first published in 1956, points to the radical nature of the changes made by the later poets and translators to the Sumerian material emphasising that, rather than 'slavishly copy' it 'they so modified its content and moulded its form, in accordance with their own temper and heritage, that only the bare nucleus of the Sumerian original remains recognisable.' These changes are especially evident in what is now considered to be the standard Sin-lique-uninni version which doesn't include early stories such as 'Inanna's Descent to the Underworld' and 'Inanna and the Huluppu Tree' (later referred to as 'Gilgamesh and the Huluppu Tree', despite Gilgamesh's secondary role in the story) but focuses more on what George Steiner calls the 'lyric masculinity' found in the Homeric epic, a genre which could plausibly have developed out of the *Gilgamesh* corpus. As Nancy Sandars comments in the introduction to her respected and popular prose version, first published in 1960 – 'it would have been historically possible for the poet of the *Odyssey* to hear stories about Gilgamesh direct, as ships from Ionia and the Islands were already trading on the Syrian coast.' Stories from Sumer about gods and goddesses and the importance of keeping them happy morphed into tales about the coming of age of young men, testosterone-driven heroes who find a kindred spirit with whom to compete in manly sports, go on adventures and undertake the quest for fame and immortality. Details, ways of telling and the textural fabric of the earlier satellite stories as part of a loosely connected cycle would surely have contributed to the cognitive cohesion of the *Gilgamesh* epic; by omitting such material the epic loses coherence.

Another reason for lack of consistency is that newly translated tablets tell the story differently. For example, the translation by Professors Andrew George and Farouk Al-Rawi of the smuggled Tablet Five (acquired by the Sulaymaniyah Museum in 2011) shows how fugitive the elements of any story can be, with Humbaba in this case being presented as a foreign potentate, rather than an ogre, and the forest itself more like a tropical jungle than a forest, with a cacophony of monkeys and parrots. As Professor George says in the appendix to his authoritative version (*The Epic of Gilgamesh*, 2003), 'The translation of fragmentary passages is often necessarily uncertain, so that the discovery of a new tablet can sometimes radically alter our understanding of the episode in question.' These anomalies can lead to flaws in the narrative. An example of this is Tablet Six where, in early stories, Gilgamesh's rejection of Inanna could be linked to power politicking among the gods; in the version we know best, it has been reduced to the actions of a powerful male putting a presumptuous woman (goddess) in her place. The subsequent episode of the killing of the Bull of Heaven was a later addition to the original, and equally shocking – although it does make a spectacular set piece to show off the two heroes' courage and skill. This seems to me to indicate a change in purpose of the text itself, from hymns extolling the glorious exploits of the deities to stories extolling the glorious exploits of men. Although women only feature as foils, they do have important parts to play in influencing events and moving the action on, as with Shamhat the 'sacred prostitute' who brings Enkidu to Uruk from the wilderness; Gilgamesh's mother, Ninsun, who persuades Shamash to protect the friends in their battle with Humbaba; the scorpion-woman who tells Gilgamesh how to run through the mountain to find his way to Uta-napishtim; Siduri, the wise woman who leads him to the boatman, Ur-shanabi; Uta-napishtim's wife who shows him where to find the Plant of Youth; and, of course, Inanna, whose actions are integral to Enkidu's death and Gilgamesh's fate.

Feminist interpretations of the *Epic of Gilgamesh* look at the battle for supremacy between Gilgamesh and Inanna/Ishtar as the evolution from a matriarchal (Earth Mother) to a patriarchal (Sun God) belief system, and this seems to me to be a possible explanation for the major shift in perception which unbalances other elements in the story. In earlier Sumerian poetry, the sacred marriage between Inanna and the king is essential to guarantee abundance. Inanna says to Dumuzi, her consort at the time, in poetry of a luminously direct and regenerative nature:

My vulva, the horn
The Boat of Heaven
Is full of eagerness like a new moon
My untilled land lies fallow.[1]

After their yearly ceremonial coupling in the temple, she blesses his reign:

As the farmer, let him make the fields fertile,
Under his reign let there be vegetation,
In the orchards may there be honey and wine
In the palace may there be long life.
May there be floodwater in the Tigris and Euphrates,
May the plants grow high on their banks and fill the meadows

Yet in Tablet Six (chapter eight in my version) when Inanna invites Gilgamesh to be her bridegroom, instead of performing the sacred rite with her to ensure the fertility of the land, the range and inventiveness of his insults is breathtaking:

You're a blade of frost scraping the ice
A broken door that lets the wind through
A cup that cuts the lip of the drinker
A shoe that bites the foot of its owner.

You're a palace that maims its own heroes
A fireplace that puts out its own fire
A fortress that slaughters its own soldiers
An elephant that kills its own mahout.

---

1 This and the poetry extract below are from *Inanna, Queen of Heaven and Earth: Her Stories and Hymns from Sumer,* Diane Wolkstein and Samuel Noah Kramer, Harper and Row Publishers, 1983.

To put the balance of male and female energies at risk in this way has a profound effect on the outcome of the story. From this point on, the narrative becomes one of loss and despair, reflected by the inhospitable barrenness of the wilderness in which Gilgamesh roams, grief-stricken after the death of Enkidu. Only at the very end when he returns, older and wiser, to carry out his duties as a king and benevolent ruler is there any hint of abundance returning to his life and to the world. He proudly shows the boatman Ur-shanabi his lifetime's achievement, the world's first city, with its citizens kept safe by the legendary wall of Uruk, made with the finest bricks and bolstered with heavy wooden joists brought (at great personal cost) from the cedar forest. Ironically, like Ozymandias, even this claim to immortality is denied as the city of Uruk with its impregnable wall is later destroyed. However, Gilgamesh does achieve the eternal life he longs for, with all the other characters in the narrative, through the epic tale of which he is the eponymous hero. My telling of the story emphasises the importance of sustaining the balance between masculine and feminine energies, and respecting both equally, in order to keep conflict and loss at bay.

My decision to tell *Gilgamesh* in different forms was to reflect the idea of many voices speaking their own version of the story – a sort of poetic heteroglossia. The forms are arranged in a loosely chiastic structure with the pivotal rejection of Inanna scene at the centre of the story in chapter eight. In some instances I have invented or expanded material, such as chapter eight where I make much more of Inanna's ascent to heaven than the original text does, using repetition (a key prosodic feature of the original epic) to suggest the covering of vast distances of time and space in order to give her character the importance I feel she deserves. In chapter ten, Enkidu's Funeral, I have used language reminiscent of the *Song of Songs*, thought to have been derived from early Mesopotamian love poetry celebrating the marriage between Inanna and Dumuzi. In the Prologue, I have gone back to the earlier Mesopotamian myth of how the world was birthed. Tiamat is the primordial goddess of the ocean, mating with the god of fresh water to produce younger deities. She symbolises the chaos of creation and is the one who gives birth to the world. I have interpreted the phrase 'He who saw the Deep, the country's foundation...' as 'He who knew how the world began.' As it is thought that the epic might have been performed as a temple piece, in chapter five, The Goddess Ninsun Prays to the Sun God Shamash, I imagined lines 21–35 being sung or chanted with music similar to the plainsong 'call and response' pattern of the Christian liturgy. There is a further sung episode in chapter eleven, Gilgamesh in the Wilderness. In chapter six, Journey to the Cedar Forest, dreams and omens were central to Mesopotamian belief systems. They interpreted dreams in various ways, sometimes, as in this chapter, the worse the dream the better the augury. Similar to Inanna's ascent to heaven in chapter eight, this chapter uses repetition to suggest the covering of geographical distance. In chapter twelve, Gilgamesh at the Edge of the World, Siduri speaks to Gilgamesh in 'eme-sal' or 'women's language'. It is not known what 'women's language' actually indicates. Gordon Whittaker in his 'Linguistic Anthropology and the Study of Eme-sal as (a) Women's Language' (2002) suggests various scenarios which range from 'a discrete women's language', an 'archaic form of Sumerian', a 'professional or class jargon', 'regional speech', 'mannered speech', 'effeminate speech' (used by men and eunuchs as well as women), 'a soprano singing voice', a 'fine speech' (used as a literary register), a 'lyrical expression' (used by poets) or even 'scribal errors'. Eme-sal is often put into the mouths of goddesses (especially Inanna) and women, but also, in a hymn, the 'Ersemma of Dumuzi', it is spoken by a female fly who says to the goddess:

> *É-kas-a-ka é-girin-na-ka dumu-mu-lu-kù-zu zu-ke-ne dè-mu-un-ti-le*
> Let the young of the wise one live in the alehouse and in the house of fruit!

No-one quite knows the significance of the stone crew of Ur-shanabi except that they are the only ones who can touch the Waters of Death and survive. Dr Salah Niazi, the distinguished Iraqi poet and *Gilgamesh* scholar, suggests that they might actually refer to some kind of Sumerian navigation system, so this is how I have interpreted them. Dr Niazi also alerted me to the filmic qualities of the *Gilgamesh* epic and several other important details. In chapter fourteen, the Plant of Youth, *gidim xul* was a malevolent ghost or demon. In this case, it represents Gilgamesh's own self-torturing demons. In chapter fifteen, Homecoming, 'Eanna' was the temple and area around it, dedicated to the presiding goddess, Inanna/Ishtar.

One of the episodes I found most problematic to understand and write was Shamhat and Enkidu's sex by the lake in chapter one, an incident fraught with cultural anachronisms. For a start, the idea of a 'holy' or 'sacred' prostitute would seem to be a contradiction in terms to a twenty-first century reader, but in ancient Sumer there doesn't seem to have been any stigma attached to sex, and certainly not to temple prostitutes in service to Inanna. They were seen as accomplished courtesans with their own acknowledged place in the temple hierarchy. Even so, being told (commanded) to trek three days into the wilderness and lie naked as a lure for a gigantic hairy wild man (probably with bad personal hygiene) seems monstrously abusive and pornographic in any century. My way of dealing with it was to interpret it as a ritual, similar to the annual symbolic couplings between Inanna's High Priestess and the king to ensure abundance in the land. In my version Enkidu approaches Shamhat gently and sings to her to reassure her; Inanna looks down on the couple, turning their lovemaking into something 'holy' or supernatural (rather than bestial). In this way I was able to imagine the scenario as having a strange, compelling lyricism – a high point, perhaps, in a festival performance with harps, lyres and temple choir, complete with eunuchs singing the counter-tenor part in eme-sal.

Acknowledgements

My thanks, first and foremost, to Stephen Knight my supervisor at Goldsmiths, London University, for helping me to bring this book into being; also to Blake Morrison and Maura Dooley at Goldsmiths; Robyn Marsack for first suggesting that I might undertake a new version of *Gilgamesh*; Arts Council England for Grants for the Arts awards to translate into Arabic, dramatise and perform extracts; the late Drue Heinz and Hawthornden Castle for a Fellowship in 2012 to study Babylonian and attempt to decipher cuneiform; Matthew Barton, Alison Brackenbury, Rebecca Farmer, Irving Finkel, Leona Medlin and Hylda Sims for help and support along the way; Martin Andrews, Euton Daley, Tom and Abigail Hawkesworth and the East Oxford Youth Choir and, particularly, Yasmin Sidhwa, Director of Mandala Theatre Company, for bringing extracts vividly to life in performance; the Helyars Poets – Fiona Benson, Julia Copus, Claire Crowther, Jane Draycott and Annie Freud – for their wisdom and insights; Tim Israel for music notation; Fran Hazelton and Dr Salah Niazi for reading and commenting on early drafts and helping me to get *Gilgamesh* into perspective; Kate Hazell for the lovely map on p. 14; Peter Francis and Louisa Yates of Gladstone's Library for shortlisting *Gilgamesh Retold* for a Gladstone's Library Award and inviting me to read at the Hearth Festival; Michael, Luke, Jazmine and Andrew at Carcanet for making my ideas into such a beautiful book; and, especially, to Adnan al-Sayegh for sharing his passion for ancient Mesopotamia with me and helping me bring the world of Gilgamesh and Inanna back to life.

Extracts have previously appeared in *And Other Poems*, *Poetry Salzburg Review*, *Raceme*, *The Gold Room*, *The Oxford Magazine*, *The Punch*, *The Sandspout*, *World English Poetry 2015*; and in *Singing for Inanna* (2014) and *The Flood* (2017) both from Mulfran Press.

Further extracts have been performed in English and Arabic as part of the Arts Council-funded 'Writing Mesopotamia' project (aimed at strengthening ties between English and Arabic-speaking communities) on BBC Radio Oxford and Resonance FM and at the British Museum, the Ashmolean Museum, Oxford, and the Enheduanna Festival of Poetry and Art 2016, Malmö, Sweden.

'The Flood' episode, from chapter thirteen and fragments from other chapters were exhibited with original prints by Frances Kiernan at the Humanitarian Dialogue Foundation of Iraq, Salam House, London, and the Iraqi Embassy (April 2017) and as part of the 'Touching Mesopotamia: Text and Texture Exhibition', Goldsmiths, London University (September-October, 2018).

I have worked from a variety of sources – mainly Andrew George's version of the *Epic of Gilgamesh* (Penguin 2003 edition with additional notes). I have also studied and compared versions by Nancy Sandars (1960), Stephanie Dalley (1989), M.G. Kovacs (1989), David Ferry (1993), B.R. Foster (2001), Stephen Mitchell (2004), Edwin Morgan (2005) and Fran Hazelton (2012). Samuel Noah Kramer's *History Begins at Sumer* (1956, 1988) and Theodore Ziolkowski's *Gilgamesh Among Us: Modern Encounters with the Ancient Epic* (2011) have proved invaluable as scholarly guides.

I am greatly indebted to Fran Hazelton, whose *Three Kings of Warka, Myths from Mesopotamia* retells the stories of Gilgamesh, his father Lugalbanda, and his grandfather Enmerkar, from translations of the original narrative texts in Sumerian and Akkadian. *Three Kings of Warka* was a product of the 'Discover Mesopotamia through Storytelling' project 2009–2012 organised by the Enheduanna Society. Fran pointed out the long process of female deities being edited out of Mesopotamian mythology as narratives were retold and developed during the 3,000 years of Mesopotamian cultural history. This corroborated my suspicions that Gilgamesh's misogynistic rant against Inanna/Ishtar (Tablet Six/chapter eight) stems from later, more patriarchal versions.